Work! Work! Work!

Contents

A Collection of Plays

Written by
**Steve Barlow
and Steve Skidmore**

Illustrated by
Shahab Shamshirsaz

Work! Work! Work!

Monsters! Heroes! Gods and Goddesses! The myths of Ancient Greece are full of these! We've always loved reading and writing about them.

One of our favourite myths is the Labours of Hercules. Hercules was half man, half god and total hero! But he could also be a bit of a naughty boy. Hercules got into trouble, BIG TIME, and as a punishment he had to perform twelve tasks (or labours). These weren't ordinary tasks like cleaning up your bedroom but nasty, probably-lose-your-life tasks.

We've taken three of our favourite labours and turned them into playscripts. We hope you like them ...

Steve Barlow and Steve Skidmore
For more information about the 2 Steves, visit their website.

Pooh!

Characters

Hercules — a hero
Homer — Hercules' friend
The King

Pooh!

A field in Greece. Enter Hercules and Homer.

Hercules   Pooh! This place smells!

Homer   You're not joking!

Hercules   Just look at the land. There's no grass anywhere — just brown stuff. What is it?

Homer   I'll give you a clue. What's brown and sounds like a bell?

Hercules	I don't know.
Homer	Dung ...
Hercules	I don't get it.
Homer	I'm wasted on you ... The brown stuff is dried dung. It's poo!
Hercules	Yuck! So what are we doing here?
Homer	We've got to wait for the King. He wants to talk to you.

Enter the king.

The king   Ah, you've arrived. I have an
interesting task for you!

Hercules   What is it?

The king   I want you to clean out the stables
where I keep my bulls.

Hercules   Clean up a bit of poo?
That sounds easy.

The king   You might think so.
But there's a catch ...

Homer   There always is.

The king	There are over five hundred of the beasts!
Hercules	Five hundred!
Homer	That's a lot of bulls.
The king	And there is something else …
Homer	There's always something else.
The king	The stables haven't been cleaned out for over thirty years!
Hercules	(*holding his nose*) Oh pooh!
The king	Correct! There's an awful lot of it! And there is another thing.
Homer	Here we go again …

The king	You've got to clean the stables in ONE day!
Hercules	Oh, double pooh!
Homer	Easy peasy!
The king	What?
Hercules	WHAT?!
Homer	Hercules doesn't need a whole day. He can do it in half a day!
Hercules	WHAT?!
The king	He hasn't got a chance.
Homer	We bet you fifty of your bulls that he can do it ...
The king	And if he doesn't?

Homer　　He'll work for you for free for the rest of the year.

Hercules　　WHAT?!

Homer　　(*whispering to Hercules*) Trust me.

The king　　I accept your bet. You'd better get moving. There's a lot of poo to clean up!

The king exits, laughing a lot!

Hercules   Look at all the poo! Why did you tell him I could do it in half a day?

Homer   Don't worry, I've got a cunning plan. Do you see those two rivers? All we have to do is ...

Homer whispers into Hercules' ear. The lights go out and dramatic music is played.

After a few minutes, the lights go up. Hercules and Homer are lying down. Enter The king.

The king   Why aren't you working?

Homer   (*yawning*) Hercules finished the job ages ago.

The king   (*in an amazed voice*) Impossible! How did he do it?

Homer   He made two holes in the stable walls. (*pointing left*) Then he dug a trench from that river.

Hercules   (*pointing right*) And a trench from that river.

Homer   And the water gushed out and cleaned away all the poo!

The king	So it wasn't Hercules who cleaned the stables, it was the river water!
Homer	Well, I suppose so, if you're going to be picky.
The king	The bet's off. You cheated so I'm not going to give you the bulls. (*He leaves.*)
Hercules and Homer	(*together*) Oh pooh!

Sky's the Limit!

Characters

Hercules — *a hero*
Homer — *Hercules' friend*
Atlas — *a Greek god*

Sky's the Limit!

*On Mount Atlas. Atlas is holding
a huge globe on his shoulders.
Enter Hercules and Homer.*

Homer	Good morning!
Atlas	What's good about it?
Hercules	You're in a bad mood.
Homer	(*to Atlas*) It looks like you've got the weight of the world on your shoulders.
Atlas	I have got the weight of the world on my shoulders. Can't you see?

Hercules	What is that thing?
Atlas	I'm holding up the sky.
Hercules	It looks like heavy work!
Atlas	Of course it is! Anyway, why are you here?
Homer	We're here to ask a favour.
Atlas	What sort of favour?
Homer	Hercules has been a naughty boy.
Hercules	And I've got to do a few tasks to make up for it.
Homer	One of the tasks is to collect three apples.
Atlas	Why can't you nip down to the shops for them?
Hercules	They're not normal apples, they're golden apples.

Homer	The golden apples are growing on a tree just over that wall.
Atlas	I know that tree. I also know that the tree is guarded by a dragon with a hundred heads!
Hercules	It was but I shot the dragon with my bow and arrow.
Homer	It's now a dead dragon!
Hercules	But I can't reach the apples.
Homer	So, could you reach up and pick three apples for us please?
Atlas	Aren't you forgetting this thing I'm holding up?
Hercules	Oh yeah ...

Atlas   If I let go, then the sky will fall and … SPLAT!

Homer   Everyone will be as flat as a pitta bread!

Atlas   Correct!

Homer   What if Hercules held the sky for you while you get the apples?

Atlas   Is he strong enough?

Hercules My muscles have got muscles.

Atlas   All right then.

Atlas hands the globe to Hercules.

Atlas   Take the weight. One, two and up!

Hercules takes the globe. Atlas goes to get the apples.

Hercules   Wow, this is heavy!

Homer   Of course it's heavy. It's the sky!

Atlas returns ...

Atlas   Here they are! Three golden apples.

Hercules   Thank you.

Homer   If you can just take the sky from Hercules, we'll be off.

Atlas	Actually, it's nice to have the weight off my back.
Hercules	Stop messing around!
Atlas	I think I'll just go on holiday.
Hercules	You can't do that! I'll get you …

Hercules tries to grab Atlas.

Homer	DON'T LET GO OF THE SKY!
Atlas	Otherwise, SPLAT! Bye, bye. Don't cry. Don't drop the sky!

Homer	Ok. That's fair enough. You need a rest. Hercules can take over.
Hercules	No I can't!
Homer	(*to Hercules*) Shhh. (*to Atlas*) But before you go, could you just hold the sky again for a minute?
Atlas	Just for a minute?
Homer	Yes, just for a minute.

Homer takes out a pillow from his bag.

Homer	I need to put this pillow between the sky and Hercules' shoulders. He's got sensitive skin.
Hercules	Have I?
Homer	Yes, you have.

Hercules hands the globe back to Atlas.

Homer   Right. Thanks for the apples! Come on Hercules, let's run for it!

Atlas   Oi! You fibbing cheaters! Come back here!

Hercules and Homer   (*together*) Bye, bye. Don't cry. Don't drop the sky!

Nice Doggy!

Characters

Hercules – a hero
Homer – Hercules' friend
Cerberus – a three-headed dog

Nice Doggy!

In the underworld. Enter Hercules and Homer.

Hercules   It's dark in here.

Homer   Of course it is. We're in Hell. It's called the underworld because it's underground!

Hercules   Oh, so that's why it's dark! Why are we here?

Homer   Because you've got to do the last of your tasks. You've got to capture Cerberus alive, and you're not allowed to use any weapons.

Hercules   Who is Cerberus?

Homer   Cerberus isn't a who, Cerberus is a what.

Hercules	What's a what?
Homer	Aren't you listening! Cerberus is a what.
Hercules	Oh. What sort of what?
Homer	Cerberus is a dog.
Hercules	So all I've got to do is capture a dog?

Homer	Cerberus isn't just any old dog. It is the dog that stops the living from getting into hell.
Hercules	That's stupid! Why would anyone who is alive want to go to hell?
Homer	I don't know! And it stops the dead from getting out of hell.
Hercules	But if they're dead, how do they get out of hell?
Homer	I don't know! Stop asking silly questions and let's find the dog.

They move forward and nearly trip over a sleeping dog.

Hercules	It's a dog! It must be Cerberus!
Homer	Shhh! Let sleeping dogs lie!

One of Cerberus' heads wakes up.

Hercules   Nice doggy.

Another of Cerberus' heads wakes up.

          Hercules   Nice doggy.

Another of Cerberus' heads wakes up.

Hercules   Er ... nice doggy ... Homer, are there three dogs here?

Homer   No! It's one dog with three heads!

Cerberus gets up and starts to bark.

Homer   Don't worry. You know the saying, 'a barking dog never bites'.

Cerberus stops barking.

Hercules   It's stopped barking.

Homer   Then it is time to worry!

Cerberus prowls nearer.

Hercules   (*in a scared voice*) Ooooh! (*to Cerberus*) Sit! There's a nice doggy ...

Homer   It's not a nice doggy. It's a nasty three-headed, razor-sharp-toothed doggy!

Hercules	I'll be friendly and give it a pat on the head. That'll stop it biting me.
Homer	You've got two hands and the dog has got three heads. One of the heads won't get patted and will start biting!
Hercules	(*to Cerberus*) Good boy. Play dead!
Homer	Fight the dog or you'll be dead and you won't be playing anything!

Cerberus leaps at Hercules. They fight!

Homer	That's it! Thump it! Watch out for its head. Not that head, the other two heads!
Hercules	Don't just stand there, help me!
Homer	Keep fighting! I've got an idea.

Homer pulls out a bag from his cloak. He creeps up behind Hercules and Cerberus.

Homer   Hold him there!

Homer drops the bag over Cerberus' three heads.

Hercules   The dog is in the bag!

Cerberus struggles as Hercules ties up the bag.

Homer   It's a doggy bag!

Hercules slings the bag over his shoulder.

Hercules: That's all of my tasks finished!

Homer   Well done! Let's go home and put the dog out.

Hercules   Good idea. I need a lie down. All these tasks have made me ...

Homer   Don't tell me, let me guess ...

Homer and Hercules   ... dog-tired!